FIREFIGHTERS TO THE RESCUE!

AMANDA NEEDS AN AMBULANCE

Written By
Kevin Bonsell

Illustrated by
Tanya Alexis

KITSAP PUBLISHING

To The Rescue! Amanda Needs an Ambulance
First edition, published 2020

Written By Kevin Bonsell
Illustrated by Tanya Alexis

Copyright © 2020, Kevin Bonsell

Hardbound ISBN-13: 978-1-952685-15-6

Published by www.KitsapPublishing.com

DEDICATION

I dedicate this book to my wife Kelly and children, Kainoa, Keahi, and Kealani. I know it's hard to have a dad that has to leave 24 hours at a time, missing birthdays, holidays, sporting events, and life's firsts. Without our solid foundation at home, I wouldn't be able to be strong at work when it's needed.

I also dedicate this book to *all* the children smiling and waving at the firefighters as we drive by in our engines and medic units.

ABOUT THE AUTHOR

For the last 20 years, Kevin Bonsell has been working as an EMT and paramedic in Maui, Hawai'i, and as a Firefighter/Paramedic for the Bremerton Fire Department. After coming home from work, he would tell real-life stories to his children, Kainoa, Keahi, and Kealani, before bedtime. His children would wait with anticipation after every shift to hear who he and his crew were able to help. This book is one of these stories.

THE FIREHOUSE DAY STARTED LIKE MANY DO.

FIREFIGHTER ROB ARRIVED AT WORK EARLY AND BEGAN TO CHECK HIS MEDIC UNIT.

Firefighter Rob made sure he had the tools needed to care for the people he would meet today. Shortly after, Firefighter Tom showed up ready to help take care of the City.

IT WAS A SUNNY SPRING MORNING AT CROWN HILL ELEMENTARY SCHOOL.

The children sprang out of class for their morning recess. Amanda and Sydney rushed to the empty playground, excited to be the first ones there. They ran as fast as they could to their favorite place on the playground—the monkey bars! Amanda was the smallest kid in her 3rd-grade class, but she was the very best on the monkey bars. She could skip bars, spin, and even do five pull-ups. Amanda and Sydney were there first, which meant they got the first trip across.

THAT WAS UNTIL
BULLY BEN
SHOWED UP.

Bully Ben was the biggest, tallest, and meanest 3rd-grader in the school.

"THESE ARE MY MONKEY BARS. BEAT IT" GROWLED BULLY BEN.

"We were here first, but we'll share them with you," said Amanda.

Bully Ben replied, "No! I said, beat it!"

"C'mon Amanda, let's just go," whispered Sydney, already walking away.

"No! I'm tired of Bully Ben always picking on everyone. I'm going to stand up to him. I'm going to challenge him to a monkey bar race!" declared Amanda.

And so she did.

BULLY BEN AGREED AND THE WHOLE CLASS GATHERED AROUND TO WATCH.

Amanda and Bully Ben lined up next to each other on the monkey bars.

Sydney said, "Ready. Set. Go!"

They were off. Amanda swept across the bars like a spider monkey. Bully Ben saw she was leading, so he reached out and grabbed her ponytail. She slipped off the bars and fell to the sand with her arms outstretched. There was a loud "snap" and a pain in her arm.

AMANDA STARTED TO CRY.

Mrs. Kepler, the 3rd-grade teacher, came running over and saw Amanda had a broken arm.

"SOMEONE CALL 911!" shouted Mrs. Kepler.

FIREFIGHTER ROB AND FIREFIGHTER TOM JUST...

...finished mopping the station floor when they heard a loud, "BEEEEEEEEEEE EEEEEEEEEEEEEEEEEEEEEEE EEEEEEEEEEEEEEEEEEEEEEEP!" followed by, "Medic 3, Medic 3, respond to Crown Hill Elementary School for an 8-year-old female with a broken arm."

The firemen jumped into their ambulance and the station door opened. Medic 3 rushed out with its lights flashing and siren blaring! All the cars pulled to the right and the neighborhood children heard the sirens and stayed far from the road. Firefighter Tom paid close attention to his driving to make sure he was safe. All the stop lights turned green and they got to the school quickly.

FIREFIGHTER TOM GRABBED THE AID BAG.

Both firefighters quickly walked over to the playground under the monkey bars where little Amanda lay holding her arm, still crying. Mrs. Kepler told Firefighter Rob what happened.

FIREFIGHTER ROB APPROACHED LITTLE AMANDA AND INTRODUCED HIMSELF.

Firefighter Rob made sure nothing else hurt besides her obviously broken arm. Firefighter Tom prepared a splint for her arm so it wouldn't move while they put her into the awaiting ambulance.

Through her tears, Amanda asked Firefighter Rob, "Am I going to be okay?"

Firefighter Rob said, "I think you broke your arm, but we are going to help you feel better. I promise." Somehow those words alone helped her relax. On the way to the hospital, Firefighter Rob gave Amanda a stuffed teddy bear … and she smiled.

ONCE AT THE EMERGENCY DEPARTMENT...

The firefighters rolled Amanda into her room, and in came her mom and dad. She wasn't crying anymore, and her parents were glad to see she was okay.

SHORTLY AFTER, DR. PERRY ARRIVED.

With a warm smile, she said, "Let's have a look."

Dr. Perry took off Amanda's splint and began to examine her arm. It hurt Amanda a little, but she didn't cry.

Dr. Perry remarked, "I think you've broken your radius and ulna. Now we need to take an X-ray to be sure, and then we'll put your arm in a cast."

The X-ray team came in and took a picture of the bones in Amanda's arm. Dr. Perry showed the picture to Amanda and her parents. Amanda was able to see right where the two bones were broken.

"A lot of children get this type of break and are able to get full use of their arm in a few months," said Dr. Perry. "You'll be just fine. Now, let's get a cast on it! What's your favorite color?"

"PINK," SAID AMANDA.

D r. Perry put the prettiest pink cast on Amanda's arm that she had ever seen.

After a long day in the ER, Amanda and her parents finally went home.

THE NEXT MORNING...

When Amanda woke up, her mommy asked her, "Would you like to stay home from school?"

"No way!" said Amanda. "I want to see my friends!"

AS AMANDA WAS GETTING OUT OF THE CAR...

Her mom handed her something strange ... a black marker! Amanda asked, "What's this for?"

"You'll see," said her mother with a smile. "Have a good day at school."

Amanda's friends were all there to greet her when she walked into the classroom. She felt so loved. Sydney declared, "I want to be the first to sign your pretty pink cast."

Now the black marker made sense! After Sydney signed, everyone in Amanda's class followed except for one boy ....

BULLY BEN SAT ALONE OUTSIDE UNDER THE TREE WITH A SAD EXPRESSION ON HIS FACE.

Am Amanda looked over and saw him and began to walk his way. Bully Ben watched her coming and looked sad and scared. When she got up next to him, he reached into his bag. And with a tear in his eye, he handed her an I'm-Sorry-Letter.

"I'm very sorry, Amanda," choked Bully Ben. "I feel horrible for being such a mean boy. It's my fault you fell and broke your arm. I'm glad you're back and okay."

Amanda replied, "I forgive you."

BULLY BEN SAID...

"I know everyone calls me Bully Ben because I am mean. I am mean because I don't have any friends. I'm not going to be mean anymore."

There was a long silence.

Amanda was shocked to hear him say this.

Amanda then smiled and said, "I'd like to be your friend. Will you sign my cast?"

With a sigh of relief and a bright smile, he signed it with three simple letters, B - E - N.

From that day on, Ben was the biggest, tallest, and nicest boy in Mrs. Kepler's 3rd-grade class.

THE END

Almost ....

TWO MONTHS LATER

The Morning recess bell rang. Amanda, Sydney, and Ben raced to the monkey bars in an effort to be the first across. The three played together on them every recess for the rest of the year. But little Amanda was still the fastest, once her pretty pink cast was off, of course.

THE END

TANYA ALEXIS DEVELOPED HER UNIQUE ARTISITC ILLUSTRATION STYLE DOING HER ROCK PAINTING WORK.

ABOUT THE ILLUSTRATOR

Tanya Alexis

Tanya Alexis is a Pacific Northwest native and is a self-taught artist who primarily paints rocks and hides them for the general public to find unexpectantly to brighten their day. Kevin Bonsell discovered Tanya by finding two of the rocks that she hid.

LIKE US

41

FAMILY FIRE SAFETY PLAN

This plan is designed to teach your family how to safely exit your home in the unlikely event of a fire.

STEP 1

PLAN YOUR ESCAPE

Draw a diagram of your home from a bird's eye view. This plan should include rooms, hallways, common areas, and exit points such as doors and windows. The purpose of this plan is for each member of the family to know where, and how, to exit the house in the event of a fire. In addition to the drawing, take time with each member of the family to practice safely exiting their room from a window, door, staircase, or ladder. While practicing, make sure that the exit point can open and is big enough for the person to safely exit.

STEP 2

CREATE A MEETING PLACE

The meeting place should be on the street side of your house. Pick a place like a tree, mailbox, swingset, or somewhere that is easy for the whole family to remember.

STEP 3

FAMILY MEETING

Have a family meeting to discuss your fire plan and to review your detailed diagram.

- Discuss the importance of family members sleeping with their doors closed. In the event of a fire, doors keep fire out.

- Locate, check, and manually sound the fire alarm/smoke detector. This will demonstrate to your family the sound a properly working fire alarm makes when triggered by smoke, heat, or fire.

- In a fire, seconds count. Discuss the importance of each family member to get themselves out. No time should be spent looking for pets, valuables, or material items.

- In the event your room is full of smoke, roll out of bed, and stay low.

- Check the door. If the door is hot, use your practiced way out. If the door is not hot, crack it open and lookout. If there's a clear path to the primary exit, take it. If not, re-shut the door and exit via your practiced route.

- Once you've safely exited your room, go to the practiced meeting place and call 9-1-1.

- Take a count of your family knowing the first question the arriving firefighter will ask is, "Is there anyone inside?" If so, "What part of the house are they located?"
- MOST IMPORTANTLY, ONCE OUT, STAY OUT!

STEP 4

PRACTICE, PRACTICE, PRACTICE FAMILY FIRE DRILL

At night, with everyone in bed and all doors closed, manually sound the fire alarm. All family members should roll out of bed, stay low, check their door for heat, exit their room from the chosen location, and meet at the previously designated meeting place.

STEP 5

HAVE A FAMILY TALK

The purpose of this drill is to prepare, not scare, young ones in the family. Make sure children understand house fires are rare.

FAMILY FIRE ESCAPE PLAN

- Draw a map of your home. Show all doors and windows.

- Visit each room. Find two ways out.

- All windows and doors should open easily. You should be able to use them to get outside.

- Make sure your home has smoke alarms. Push the test button to make sure each alarm is working.

- Pick a meeting place outside. The place should be in front of your home. Everyone will meet at the meeting place.

- Make sure your house number can be seen from the street.

- Talk about your plan with everyone in your home.

- Learn the emergency phone number for your fire department.

- Practice your home fire drill frequently!

- Make your own home fire escape plan using the grid provided on the following pages.

SAMPLE FIRE ESCAPE PLAN

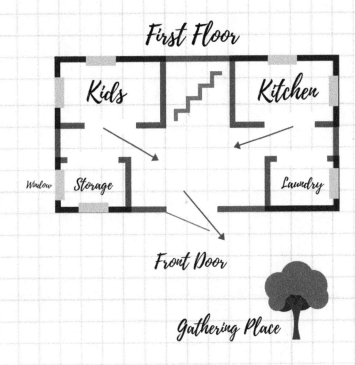

First Floor

Kids

Kitchen

Window Storage

Laundry

Front Door

Gathering Place